Blooming Us

Blossoming Poetry..

Kane Benjamin Crookes

Grosvenor House
Publishing Limited

All rights reserved
Copyright © Kane Benjamin Crookes, 2024

The right of Kane Benjamin Crookes to be identified as the author
of this work has been asserted in accordance with Section 78
of the Copyright, Designs and Patents Act 1988

The book cover is copyright to Kane Benjamin Crookes

This book is published by
Grosvenor House Publishing Ltd
Link House
140 The Broadway, Tolworth, Surrey, KT6 7HT.
www.grosvenorhousepublishing.co.uk

This book is sold subject to the conditions that it shall not, by way of
trade or otherwise, be lent, resold, hired out or otherwise circulated
without the author's or publisher's prior consent in any form of
binding or cover other than that in which it is published and
without a similar condition including this condition being
imposed on the subsequent purchaser.

A CIP record for this book
is available from the British Library

ISBN 978-1-83615-039-8

Table of Contents

Notes vii
Acknowledgements.. xi
Introduction.. xiii

'Red Strawberry' 1
'Subtle Piano Keys' 2
'All Hallows Eve' 3
'Nature at its T' 4
'Hazel Gaze' 5
'Fallen From the Tree' 6
'In the Soil' 7
'A Pale Canvas' 8
'Sa*n*d' 9
'Could Free Verse' 10
'Cotton Threads' 11
'Meadow Blooms and Heddle Looms' 12
'O White Rose' 13
'Wistful Stars' 14
'Carried' 15
'Hung' 16
'Stars' 17
'W*o*ven' 18
'Daffodils' 19

'Petals' 20
'The Moon, the Sun, at Noon' 21
'Strikes' 22
'Leaves Blow' 23
'Rain' 24
'Salad Green' 25
'Branches' 26
'Sunkissed' 27
'Daisy' 28
'Spiderwebs' 29
'Umbrellas' 30
'It was the Sound of the Opera' 31
'Snow' 32
'Glass' 33
'Green' 34
'Sticks' 35
'Cotton' 36
'Paper Moon' 37
'Petals Like Emeralds' 38
'Foggy' 39
'Twilight' 40
'Robin's Claw' 41
'Branches, and Leaves' 42
'Like a CAN-vas' 43
'Pansies' 44
'Lily Petals' 45

'Waxen'	46
'Roses, Noses'	47
'Frame'	48
'Clock'	49
'The Cerulean Beads'	50
'Dandelions'	51
'Strawberries'	52
'Canterbury Bells'	53
'Iris'	54
'A Rose Grins'	55
'Apple Blossom'	56
'Red Turns Brown'	57
'Red Buttons'	58
'A Daffodil'	59
'Placed'	60
'Pineapple'	61
'The White Lilac'	62
'Red Poppies'	63
'Poet's Narcissus'	64
'Apples and Quinces'	65
'The White and Red Rose'	66
'Peppermint'	67
'Leaves and Berries'	68
'Globe Thistle Wands'	69
'Noon, Evening, Night'	70
About the Author	71

Notes

In Roland Barthes's Essay *The Death of the Author* (1967), we distinguish "it is language which speaks" and not the author. I keep-in-mind this statement within my poetry which you will find by the frequent use of the metonymy. For instance, let's consider the noun 'Oak' from my poem *Candy Floss* – or candy floss for 'clouds' let's say, which you will find in this book. The simplicity of the fresh metaphor almost acts imperatively as it seemingly exclaims the verb "cease". CEASE! And absorb nature and natural things. Again, I quote 'cease' as it seems the most appropriate. That is, in a soothing cacophony, for the audience to pause and determine using both the individual heart and mind whether it be metonymically employed for a *Tree* or for a *Coffin*. They are both primarily known as oakwood, and oak opens doors in which one can walk.

You may be intrigued as to why I quote "fresh metaphors" – I quote this, as, it is an imagistic technique of the fellow American modernist poet Ezra Pound. I have taken up inspiration from his works over the course of my current university degree at Manchester Metropolitan University. Since then, I have delved into various of his *selected poems* throughout his life. Pound achieved his target-from-the-source as he 'compressed' *In a Station of the Metro* to a nineteen syllabic haiku: a two-liner image which nails the context of his fleeting melancholy inside a Paris

Metro's Concorde station. The simplicity of 'petals' and a 'bough' and the natural colour of 'black' are what describes this experience to which I was instantly drawn. Indeed, like 'red' in my allegorical 'Red Strawberry' – or unstructured ballad of metaphorical resonance when considering the switching musicality.

"Sucked and sucked and/Spoiled and f*cked" – this course of polysyndeton, I suppose you could view like the heightening of rhythm on the Piano. The more fingers on the keys, the more complex is the melody, provided which side. Again, I quote 'which side' for the poem to resonate with self. Like Christina Rossetti's *Goblin Market*, the parallel lines of temptation: "Apples and Quinces, Lemons and Oranges, Plump Unpecked Cherries, Melons and Raspberries" can be read for Laura's sexual temptation into which she gives, when considering the theme of the Fallen Woman, which was the result of a male-dominated Victorian canon where the female mouth was shut. Provided there is no fixed canon of today, I was nevertheless inspired by her melody and thus incorporated her 'beat'. You will also find the verb "sucked" in her poem.

A lot of my haiku, however, holds the traditional structure of five/seven/five syllables. I think this is ironic to my love for Pound's poetry as he says to not rely on strict syllable counts in haiku when it comes to the imagistic technique. However, the term "fresh metaphors" which was originally derived from T.E Hulme's Essay,

'Romanticism and Classicism' I feel paints images and tells a story in a fleeting manner whether the structure deviates from the traditional syllable count or not. I suppose you would find nuances within the enjambed lines or by rhyme. Inspiration from William Wordsworth will be found in the intertextual referencing of Daffodils.

Acknowledgements

Firstly, I would like to acknowledge my close friends and family for their unmatched support throughout my written journey. Particularly my parents, and grandparents, Barbara and William for all the financial support along.

I'd like to mention some friends who are on my degree in Manchester: Elisha Singh, Grace Gorman, and Megan Elizabeth Hall, for having all been amazing friends throughout and sharing many memorable memories with. Grace, I will forever treasure the vintage copy of A Christmas Carol you bought me; I am in love with the paper. Elisha, I will hold close our 'berylling' around the park come midnight; and the embarrassment from you asking me to read aloud my poems.

You will find Megan on Instagram @writingwithroses who also occasionally showcases her talent – go check her out! Thank you, Megan, for all your uplifting support, and I hope you never stop writing lovely work!

I have had endless support on social media from many poets across the world; not just poets, but people who take their time to recognise, read and find a sense of belonging in whichever poems I choose to put out into the public. I have taken great inspiration from German Poet, Ena @ enapepena since the beginning of my writing. She is an extremely talented woman who has an unmatchable commitment to her work and never fails to impress us.

Her poems hold a particular melody, and an encapsulating use of vocabulary. I can image her works being bestselling one day and her being recognised as the new Shakespeare's sister.

Thank you, Ena, for your support and helping me realise my writing potential.

My best friend Ava Crowther and cousin Amber I would like to thank. Ava, for being a best friend and more so having to watch me write as soon as I get the urge during our time abroad. You are an amazing lady who is deserving of every blessing in life. Amber, for showing her love for my poetry with her with her love for literature, and for being the best cousin I could ever have.

Lastly, I would like to thank the English department at MMU for the course to which you are so dedicated: I have been able to 'shape' myself and find out what I am most passionate about.

Introduction

Since the recent death of my great-grandmother, Daisy, life's destiny has been put into perspective. I'd assume it is pursuing what your soul desires with steadfast dedication and not holding back; that is, before you haven't a choice. It turns out my choice was poetry. I've never acknowledged how grief was supposed to feel then; but with Daisy being a flower, my recent love for employing nature into poetry to make nature poetry, I feel is noteworthy. Initially, my memory was the epitome of the first-ever pieces I'd write. I remember exploring what I 'like' to write and found a comfort in nature as I strolled down my trip to Oranjestad, Aruba. You could possibly guess, with the juxtaposed snow-like sand, sea and palm tree, that this, say, chokehold serenity turned my brain into a snowflake. I say snowflake, as despite the innocence of one that would melt onto your palm during the time at which it lands, there's also an association with coldness at the desolate centre of such irregular avenues. I'd say like the coldness of my mind that was the centre of my poems. Love and the complexities, and so on.

Exploring the themes 'mind', and love, nature inevitably became a great metaphor for the poems which you will notice as you read. It resulted in me delving into the nineteenth century language of flowers. Specifically, I noticed in the Victorian era that nature was used biblically and not just because of the Victorian love for nature – or the "freshness of the early world" as Matthew Arnold quoted, having interconnected his feelings to the ebb and flow of the sea in his poem *Dover Beach*. When I say biblically, I mean Laura's biblical sinning for giving into temptation in Rossetti's *Goblin Market*: the order of the Goblins' fruits on sale gradually becomes sinister. Although this era has long passed, I incorporated this type of sinister ideal in a contemporary manner. For example, I used a red strawberry as a metaphor for addiction or attachment and derived what could be told from the fruit; the cacophony of love in the sense of being left in a situation where such feelings are unreciprocated: being "f*cked" to the "tangling depths of grass" like a noose. The art of free verse is what allowed me to express the beat, or experience, freely.

In terms of the imagistic technique, particularly mine, I used the vividness of my imagination to make words fresher. For example, taking inspiration from *In a Station of the Metro* where Pound seems to 'paint' what he sees in the Paris Metro Concorde Station, I did the same during my time in Budapest. For example, it was in Budapest's Metro where I painted my poem *It was the Sound of the Opera*, a fleeting melancholy with the ghostlike faces that were seen through the windows. The title I'd say is metonymically employed for something such as: *It was the Circle of Life*. Specifically, painting a sense of modern-day life that exudes the troubles that people face day-to-day, or conveys the troubles, depending on the way in which it is interpreted. Indeed, I utilised this approach to poetry consistently throughout my time there. Another poem, *Spiderwebs* is subject to the Danube River, highlighting its blood-curdling historical context of the Second World War. During 1944, Jewish citizens were lined up and shot into the river at the point where the shoes lie. I suppose you could draw in historical contexts to many of the poems. Anyway, I hope you enjoy reading; finding solace by resonating with the poetry; and the mere comfort of nature imagery.

'Red Strawberry'

Red strawberry easy to find
Sweet and ripe are one of a kind
During the day
Enduring the may
Bless-ed by a uniquely juice
To be
Sucked and sucked and
Spoiled and fucked
To the
Tangling depths of grass
Like a noose
Loose, of the choked neck
After a bite or two to rot
Brightly lightly green
Unknowingly horrifyingly it seems
Like there could be fire
The middle of the moon
Not the sun
Lying, let he
On a bittersweet noon

Noir, his writing
Colour, his biting
For fun

'Subtle Piano Keys'

A moustache frowns in its silence
Like red ribbons for stitches
Dripping with blood
Tied to his curious lips
Reflected by his bedside
Mirror in front; like
Instructions—instructing him on
The song: his choice to play
On the subtle piano keys
That rest and grin during
Night and day;
Black as his raincoat
But as white as his shirt's collar
Like sticks of liquorice
Surrounded by the sherbet
Once combined it sure as hell can be sour
But sucked the more can be a heavenly-sweet sugar

'All Hallows Eve'

hands are wrapped up in black leather;
in black gloves for the bittersweet weather,
two fingers hold and smoke a rolled cigarette,
dropping the quarterly butt to the floor,
another one to forget;
alight and rolling,
the gust of regularly winds keep smoking,
the brown contents that are so little left,
scattered irregularly blazing coffee and orange;
the crisp air spins them a ball,
like casting a nature spell,
with someone yet to tell;

the nearest puddle,
containing soggy, wet leaves,
so happens to be petrol,
spilled *for All Hallows Eve.*

'Nature at its T'

The suns beams will gift a glow onto the bark of the tree,
Like the oil paint coated brush when it meets the canvas,
The rain will flood the eerie half-lit street,
Like tears that blacken her white face when they smear and smudge her eyeliner,
In a cycle oftentimes unknowingly,
Unknowingly as each passing bird of any kind and when it comes to collect its prey,
Whether be unkindly,
Or fascinating to one's eye,

That is nature,
From the 'N' to the 'T'—
Nature at its T.

'Hazel Gaze'

Hazel eyes gaze the autumn morning sun,
Beaming figures are out on the run,
The oh what has just sprinted past the path;
Beyond my feet,
Is the chestnut squirrel with its nut to eat, though
Soon disappeared among the tawny, shedding trees;
So disguised from what appears a thousand, thousands of leaves
Like a canvas splashed crazily orange and brown paint
Pinned with withered moths,
Enough to make you faint.

'Fallen From the Tree'

Walnuts on the land
Fallen from the tree
The pineapple in the hand
Picked so fresh, now free
For the pricks to prick
The palms from which they
Bleed from the flesh so free
For it to drop and split
In half—or in quarters of three,
Exposing fresh its flesh
Like the freshest
Of fruits you could see:
Glistening and watery.
Water the mouth, for me

'In the Soil'

Love, confess your crime
As you sever
My throat and leave a gaping scar
Sewing my eyes shut
Of what hideously bleeds
Yet you keep my brain alive to ponder
Like the dead buried alive
Like a disabling disability is
The possibility of one and
The next from what I give;
Suffocating beneath the pouring soil,
Six feet under: my thunder
Contained in such pretty
Spruce lumber, but
Breaking away and going through
All the roots and loops
Like a Ferris wheel
Like cartwheels
Like an anaemic clown spinning its balls to
The rhythmic chiming: the circus tune
In the soil, which grows a daisy if no rose
But passes us: bones to
Reach an earthly earth and
Not one that succumbs
At my feet

Love: *the tombstone*
Resting on your life

'A Pale Canvas'

A pale canvas stands tall and
Is so hungry
For colour art and money
For a tougher heart, sweet honey
She gasps with ribbons tied to
Her hair shining bright
Like seaweed, green and blue
At the canvases fire orange and red
Abstract for her fellow angels
Birthed onto the flame, now dead
Yet live everlasting long through
Cotton ball and thread—for eyes
And colour and paint and money
Her horse trots along in a hurry.
Rest now, *sweet honey*

'Sand'

Sand, you rest
Like a tree in its mighty roots
So softly yet
Hold the ability
To whirl your
Grains and contents into a spiral
Like a whirlpool in
A sea of water
When the storm occurs
So suddenly
And prove somehow there's no
Cacophony
Without the euphony
In what begins with 'S'

'Could Free Verse'

Could free verse
Be a poet's curse?
How we are able
To bleed our ink
In the simplest ways
Like a droplet of rain
Dropping from the
Petal of the rose blessed
Moitié rouge et moitié noir
After being soaked by rain
Is it enough, the
Imagery enough to leave a scar?
Like the one on his tongue
Seen so long and longer
The more he tells his tale
How it can become so pale
Ways in which can make you
See whatever you end with, too

'Cotton Threads'

The pitch-black buttons
That hang from cotton threads, are
Like beetles, seen only with their heads
Found in some woods, near his woodland bed
In which bullets scream beyond the
Baby deer stood near to the pond, but there's
The lily on the beck, for which is he fond;
Above seems a thousand suns
That would light up a ribbon or bun
Though the black button,
Coming fourth, is the nun

'Meadow Blooms and Heddle Looms'

The grass in spring: the meadow blooms
And sits the passé with heddle looms
The daisy smiles and wraps the fingers
Lazy is miles away and traps the thinkers
The red rose lies with his dimples, but
The black rose dies a cold symbol
An apple so green, blended in its tree
Happily fallen, clean, tasted by tongue
And marked with teeth, for hours long
And the moon hanged again.

'O White Rose'

    O white rose
O lily on the grass like frost
Which woven white silk

'Wistful Stars'

Wistful stars shine
Bright and some draw a line
And seven more
As the sea meets the shore
Reaches for the moon
Like a town of white teeth

'Carried'

Candy floss for clouds
Cry heavily, very loud
Crashes, the birdie's tail
Lets the rose be alight
And from red to black
It dances and wails
Heard from near oak
Is her fixtures, so hollow
Thuds down is her pale hand
On the bedside table, in sorrow
And florid as the coffin
Is carried.

'Hung'

Night-time hung its tapestry
Above the silhouette—a tree
Sits beautifully black beneath
Stars brushed glittery white
As the earthly breeze spells
Upon us a deathly cold fright
As the moon shines orange is
A Chinese lantern at its peak
Like a parrot tulip that does
Not dance unless the weather
Is hot and still—her lips are blue
And just love-sick feverish dew

'Stars'

The stars sing you a lullaby
The moon acts a pillow for the night-sky
A spillage of black glitter
On the paper—artist and writer's
Wicked ink poured black or blue
Skies and sunshine spells
The yellow rose floats fever-dew
In the river—by passers don't miss
Along with the bellflower that
Swam up near and gave a kiss
Despite the stars that hung
Red and orange as he sung

'Woven'

A melting sun during dusk
A rising sun enduring dawn
The moon is hung—born
In autumn, like a white bow
On a tux stained with the
Finest red wine spilled mixed
With the fruitiest tropical juice
The squirrels are now loose
Is the sunflower in the wind-y
As those mediums scream
From the canvas as a dead moth
Is frozen with frost—pinned are
Those *woven* cloths and—leaves
Will rise again during spring

'Daffodils'

Above the hills
Below the skies
I watch beyond the glaze
Those dancing daffodils

I close the curtains, and
Shot me is their eyes
As in these bricks—lies
Those haunting daffodils

In solitary bliss
A daffodils kiss, is—

'Petals'

A basket of fresh petals
Are thrown in the air
Rains down fresh blood
Rushes from head to toe
And I put on my finest bow

'The Moon, the Sun, at Noon'

The moon, the sun, at noon
Orders me a bow—two
Pencils to shade my *sketch*
A flower, for words *fetched*

'Strikes'

The sun strikes the railway
Ignites an innocent fire
Inside of me—as my eyes
Black buttons—they stare

'Leaves Blow'

The leaves blow me away
From the door—night, day
With them—they s*warm* my mind
And a flower grows from my eyes

'Rain'

I collect rain with my hands
Seep *blood*—spoiling the grass
Bleeds like *wine* due cracked glass
Presents a child—rubber bands

'Salad Green'

The air blows salad green
Leaves—*tomato* roses, *yellow* daffodils
Dance in a line up those hills
Reaching far—thus the flower float

'Branches'

The freezing branches *(melt)*
In spring during—*thunder*
Sparks fire from the blue—*under*
The sun wrapped—*a blanket*

'Sunkissed'

Sickly airs during storms
Blow a stalk—its thorns
Like vines on a wrist
And my chin is sun-kissed

'Daisy'

A daisy smiling on the path
Is warm, stricken—the sun
Strikes—*crazily* arrays—light
And I'm—the shade for *days*

'Spiderwebs'

The legs that stood knitting
Like berry baskets
Outside—the glass at which it shouts
Hung the whitest spider, webs,
Like pale cloths
And the Danube was at its wildest ebb

'Umbrellas'

The night-time hung
Over me like a thousand
Umbrellas—yet the sand
Is wet—the spades no more
A letter washed up to shore
Better—than the snowflake,
The moon—ever before

'It was the Sound of the Opera'

Anaemic faces
melt like cubes of
ice—glazes
appearing from
the black—
tracks jolted like
instruments in
and suddenly
there were the
thousand gloves
after the Opera—

'Snow'

A pool full of
wistful stars for
teeth—of the
snow children
and there was the
polaroid—yellow
flowers and
amelloides—the
blanket for
warmth

'Glass'

And a ghost hung himself on the glass; Floral tapestry—one hundred white flowers—bloom in the coming bowers

'Green'

I sat on green, and
Above me was blue
Flew past was the
Propellers—the flowers had
Jolt and the clouds were cut
For the sun was new, and
There was a feather—
Passing: the bowers,
By passers, passers by
Inhaled

'Sticks'

The sticks tower over,
Fallen are those few,
Two died of the sun
Competes with the moon
In Royal summer

'Cotton'

All the souls bleed from
  The soulless light
  Paints the conquest
  Behind the cotton—
Candy provided the sun

'Paper Moon'

The sky washed over like a river
On which the moon floated like paper—
Cuts, full circle—they danced around
The petals, sang for the nettles
Suddenly no where, to be found

'Petals Like Emeralds'

Petals stared like emeralds—
Nature's own labyrinth
Is the spider's web—
Rain*drops*
Ribcage, catastrophe
The cigarettes—brazen, the shed

'Foggy'

Branches sing silhouettes;
The *church* and the thousands—
Leaves, lest we forget
Due the sky is *foggy*

'Twilight'

Twilight *struck* the path—
Golden stones, due wrath
Screams, these yellow seams
And daisies smile by all means

'Robin's Claw'

The fragments of the net
Stands the Robin's claw
Those leaves on the tree
Sing a melody at the door

'Branches, and Leaves'

Branches are molten
The leaves are woven—
Fabrics—sewn—tough
At the seams, buttercups

Blow in winds, rough
Is the bark's touch
Kisses the flower whilst
Playing in the park

'Like a CAN-vas'

Taken me was the grass
Like a canvas sharp, green
Is the stalk on the rose,
But raindrops on my nose

'Pansies'

Pansies resting green and *blonde*
Like the sun—the sunniest day
Strikes the bush—berries; red, bland,
Like stars for which twinkle, the Milky Way

'Lily Petals'

Buttons plucked from the shirt;
Lily petals, brushed over the dirt

'Waxen'

Lilies sing in noon
Like a moon's tired—
Eyes due *birdsong*
But waxen is *this, song*

'Roses, Noses'

Baskets of roses,
Those hanging
Travel upwards, noses,
Snort the daisies
Those gOldenrods spinning
Like spinning tops—
But those scarlet—
Stools

'Frame'

The oil screamed
From the frame,
Slipped in fame—was
The jewels through which
The blue shines
Above the shrines—are the
The ivy's tossed
The pages, turned liquorice
White

'Clock'

The clock hung red;
A crescent of time
Like the moon after
Water, lemon, lime
Are the gardens—it's
Juxtaposed of golden

'The Cerulean Beads'

The cerulean beads,
On the rope,
Hung, dropped and
Sewn again
Was the poppy, blood-red
Pools, the grass, champagne

'Dandelions'

A river knocked on the
Spruce with magic twigs
So I dipped in my finger
And I was shot with
Electrolysis—the
Dandelions sailed like
Blood clots twinkling my
blood, Like stars, and
Seemed to linger, longer,
Lighter, the sun, another,

'Strawberries'

Strawberries kiss us
On the tongue so fruitfully
They taste bittersweet

'Canterbury Bells'

Canterbury bells
Chime under the moon and sun
Finest summers day

'Iris'

Iris springs out like
A pearlescent purple pearl
Their leaves frown upon

'A Rose Grins'

A rose grins colour
Like a yellow marguerite
Two wild roses

'Apple Blossom'

Apple blossom: a
Floral tapestry—cotton
Threaded in the rain

'Red Turns Brown'

Red carnations turn
Brown during wilt with a weep
A soul masterpiece

'Red Buttons'

Red buttons are placed
Through the green cotton—threaded
Sewing a red rose

'A Daffodil'

A Daffodil is
Handed, regarding such
Blooming Eglantine

'Placed'

Placed on the red wall
In the hall, a tapestry
Fire, spindle tree

'Pineapple'

A Pineapple is
Picked like a scarlet Apple
Blood seeps down the hands

'The White Lilac'

The white Lilac is
Coupled with the white Lily
The purest emblems

'Red Poppies'

A red poppy is
Threaded with a sharp needle
Worn for the poppies

'Poet's Narcissus'

This writing is not
Bad for one in red ribbons
Poet's narcissus

'Apples and Quinces'

Apples and quinces
But lemons and oranges
Oh, the tastiest

'The White and Red Rose'

The white and red rose
Blowing on the salad grass
Utility, them

'Peppermint'

A peppermint blows
In cold—colder—coldest air
Ready to be picked

'Leaves and Berries'

Leaves and berries fall
From the tall mulberry tree
It is getting cold

'Globe Thistle Wands'

Globe thistle wands picked
Your eyes follow those blue bells
Magic now happens

'Noon, Evening, Night'

Skies are blue in noon
The sun melts in the evening
The white rose at night

About the Author

Hi! I hope you enjoyed the collection; it has been an honour to share my work you all. I now want to share with you a bit about myself and my life.

My name is Kane Crookes, I am twenty years old from Sheffield, United Kingdom, and I am currently reading English Literature at Manchester Metropolitan University.

I have been writing consistently since the age of nineteen. Though I have wrote pieces here and there throughout my childhood; I've decided they will remain private; they are in the bin. Initially, what inspired me was entering the 2023 Manchester Poetry Prize hosted by The Manchester Writing School. It is almost like something 'clicked' and poetry came so naturally. I didn't win the competition, however; it is the subjectivity and judgement of words which makes it nonetheless enjoyable and is my drive to write more and more. I cannot see myself ever stopping writing poetry.

I am influenced by personal experiences and the beauty of the natural world. Entwining mind and memories, people with nature, stimulates that part of mind and sends shivers up my tree. It is almost like looking at a flower with three petals and viewing it as a tapestry: a sonnet of adoration, which is suddenly a haiku.

It was in Cambridge where I truly got to explore my creativity. Recently, I chose to conduct a weekend course at the University of Cambridge Institute of Continuing Education, Madingley Hall. The prettiest gardens welcomed the purest emblems. You will find reference to Cambridge in this book, particularly in my poem *The Cerulean Beads.*

www.ingramcontent.com/pod-product-compliance
Lightning Source LLC
Chambersburg PA
CBHW032010080426
42735CB00007B/555